AT THE FARM

David M. Schwartz *is an award-winning author of children's books, on a wide variety of topics, loved by children around the world.* Dwight Kuhn's *scientific expertise and artful eye work together with the camera to capture the awesome wonder of the natural world.*

For a free color catalog describing Gareth Stevens Publishing's list of high-quality books and multimedia programs, call 1-800-542-2595 (USA) or 1-800-461-9120 (Canada). Gareth Stevens Publishing's Fax: (414) 225-0377. See our catalog, too, on the World Wide Web: gsinc.com

Library of Congress Cataloging-in-Publication Data

Schwartz, David M.
　　At the farm / by David M. Schwartz; photographs by Dwight Kuhn.
　　　　p. cm. — (Look once, look again)
　　Includes bibliographical references (p. 23) and index.
　　Summary: Introduces, in simple text and photographs, the characteristics of
some of the animals that can be found on a farm. Includes a sheep, rooster,
mouse, goat, pig, horse, and duckling.
　　ISBN 0-8368-2221-8 (lib. bdg.)
　　1. Livestock—Juvenile literature. 2. Animals—Juvenile literature. [1. Domestic
animals.] I. Kuhn, Dwight, ill. II. Title. III. Series: Schwartz, David M.
Look once, look again.
SF75.5.S35　1998
636—dc21　　　　　　　　　　　　　　　98-15405

This North American edition first published in 1998 by
Gareth Stevens Publishing
1555 North RiverCenter Drive, Suite 201
Milwaukee, Wisconsin 53212 USA

First published in the United States in 1997 by Creative Teaching Press, Inc., P. O. Box 6017, Cypress, California, 90630-0017.

Text © 1997 by David M. Schwartz; photographs © 1997 by Dwight Kuhn. Additional end matter © 1998 by Gareth Stevens, Inc.

Printed in the United States of America

1 2 3 4 5 6 7 8 9 02 01 00 99 98

AT THE FARM

by David M. Schwartz

photographs by Dwight Kuhn

A SPRINGBOARDS INTO

SCIENCE

SERIES

Gareth Stevens Publishing

MILWAUKEE

What has woolly curls all over its b-a-a-a-a-ck?

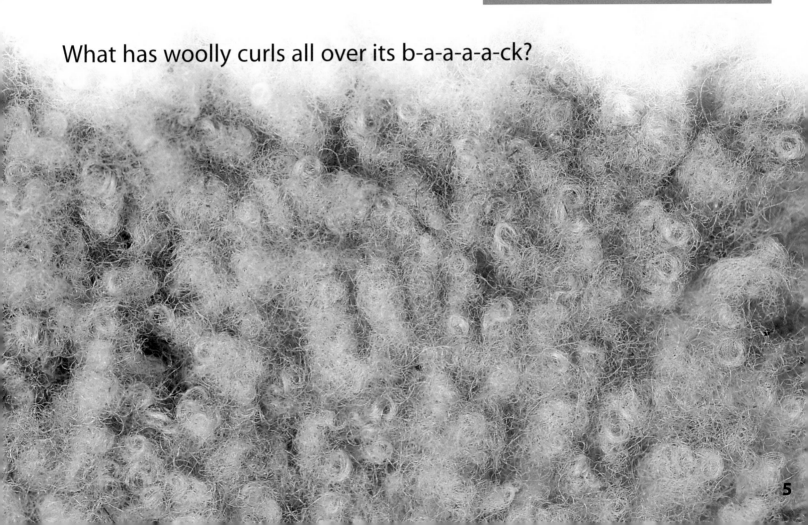

Sheep have thick, woolly coats that help keep them warm in winter. In spring, the farmer cuts off the sheep's wool. It can be made into sweaters and coats to help keep you warm in winter, too.

6

Would you believe this is a comb?
It's not the kind of comb you use on your hair!

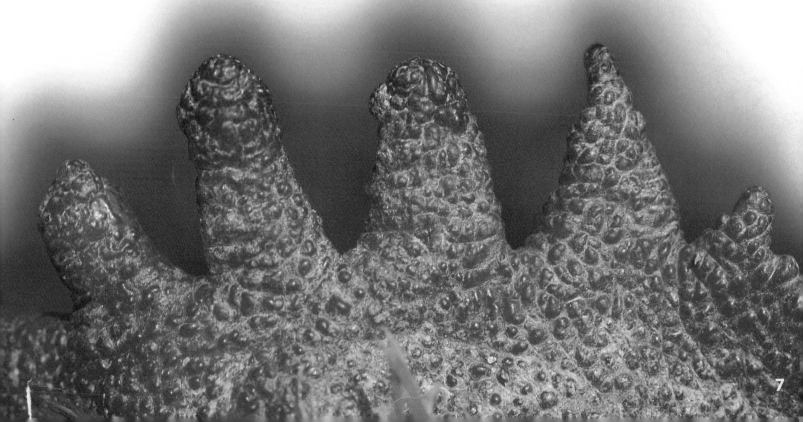

The rooster, a male chicken, has a bright red comb on top of his head. The hen, a female chicken, also has a comb, but it is smaller. Chickens recognize each other by their combs.

Heat escapes from the combs because they are not covered with feathers. This helps chickens cool off in hot weather.

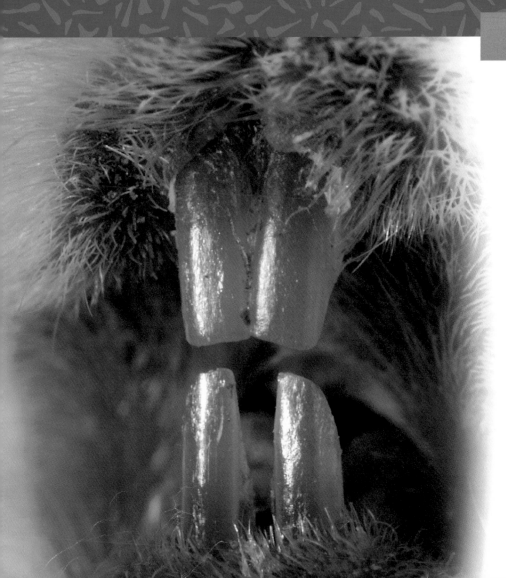

These strong, sharp teeth
belong to a little animal
that's meek as a . . .

…mouse. With their sturdy teeth, mice gnaw through hard seeds. They often eat the grain meant for cows, pigs, and other farm animals.

Almost every farmer has barn mice. That is why many farmers also have barn cats!

This kind of horn is for butting, not for blowing!

In the wild, goats fight fiercely with their horns. But in the barnyard, one goat butts another to say, "Get out of my way!" As a goat grows bigger, its horns grow bigger, too.

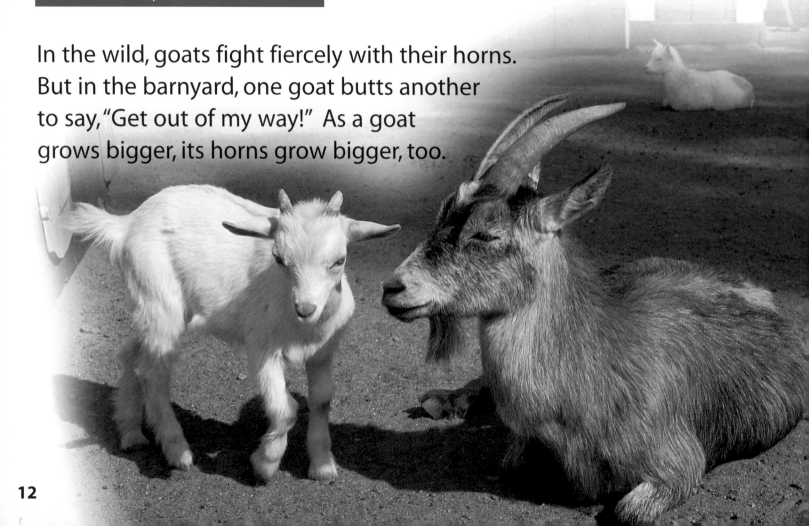

You might ride on the back of this animal. Flies do, too. Swish goes the tail. Shoo fly, shoo!

13

LOOK AGAIN

A horse's tail makes a great flyswatter.

With its sharp front teeth, a horse bites off blades of grass. The horse chews the grass with its flat back teeth.

14

What has a flat, round nose that digs in the dirt? Can you "sniff" out the answer?

Pigs root through the dirt with their noses for things to eat. They have a very good sense of smell. In hot weather, pigs wallow in the mud to cool off.

First, this is an "egg cracker."
Then it grows into a
little "quacker."

A duckling uses a sharp "egg tooth" on its little bill to crack the eggshell open as it hatches. The egg tooth soon falls off because the duckling no longer needs it.

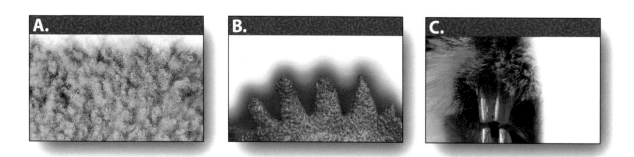

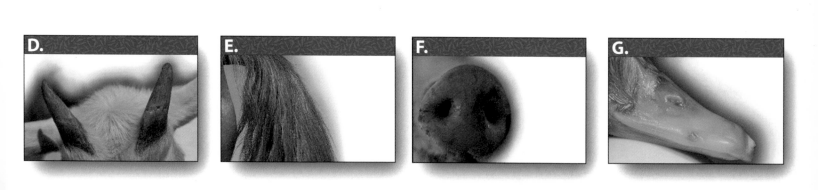

Look closely. Can you name these animals?

LOOK AGAIN

A.

Sheep

B.

Rooster

C.

Mouse

D.

Goats

E.

Horse

F.

Pigs

G.

Ducklings

How many were you able to identify correctly?

blade: a single piece of grass.

butting: hitting or pushing with the head or horns. Goats sometimes butt one another.

comb: the brightly colored crest on the top of an adult chicken's head. The hen has a much smaller comb than the rooster.

duckling: a young duck.

egg tooth: the sharp point on a duckling's bill that is used to crack open the eggshell.

gnaw: to chew or bite.

grain: the small, hard seeds of plants, such as wheat, corn, or rice, that can be eaten.

hatch: to break open, or emerge; for example, from an egg.

hen: an adult female chicken.

horn: a hard, bony growth on the head of some animals, such as sheep and goats.

meek: timid; not resisting or fighting back.

recognize: to know someone or something.

rooster: an adult male chicken.

root (v): to dig in the earth with the snout or nose, like a pig does.

sturdy: strong; well-built.

swish: to move with a soft, rustling motion.

wallow: to roll around in mud.

woolly: covered with wool or another soft material.

Activities

Horning In

At the library or on the Internet, find photographs of various horned animals, such as buffalo, pronghorn, antelope, sheep, goats, giraffes, and rhinoceroses. How are the horns alike or different from each other in size, shape, material, and number? Draw a world map, and mark where each type of horned animal makes its home.

Built-In Tools

A horse's tail can be used as a flyswatter. Can you think of other "built-in tools" that animals have? Make a list, starting with farm animals and then adding other animals. Can you think of a part of an animal's body that can be used like a saw? A nutcracker? A chisel? A rake? A shovel? Visit a garden center or hardware store to help you with ideas.

Farm Hunt

Wool that is used in sweaters and other clothing comes from sheep, which live on farms. Go on a search around your house for all the different products that come from farms, such as cheese, ice cream, eggs, clothing, and so on. Cotton is another natural material that comes from a farm. Is it from an animal or a plant?

Barnyard Charades

Play a game of charades with friends by acting out different farm animals. Think of twenty different animals that live on a farm, and write their names on separate slips of paper. Put the names in a bag, and take turns picking one. Act like the animal, and see if your friends can guess which animal you are imitating.

More Books to Read

Farm Animals. Animals At a Glance (series). Isabella Dudek (Gareth Stevens)
Fuzzy the Duckling. Real Baby Animals (series). Gisela and Siegfried Buck (Gareth Stevens)
Great American Horses. Victor Gentle and Janet Perry (Gareth Stevens)
Magnificent Horses of the World (series). Hans-Jörg Schrenk (Gareth Stevens)
Woolly Sheep and Hungry Goats. Allan Fowler (Childrens Press)
The World of Mice. Virginia Harrison (Gareth Stevens)

Videos

Animals (series). (Churchill Media)
The Horse. (Barr Films)
Look Again (series). (Bullfrog Films)
A Visit to the Farm. (New World Video)

Web Sites

zebu.cvm.msu.edu/~dawsonbr/welcome.htm
www.ics.uci.edu/~pazzani/4H/Sheep.html

Some web sites stay current longer than others. For further web sites, use your search engines to locate the following topics: *agriculture, chickens, cows, ducks, farming, horses, pigs,* and *sheep.*

INDEX